.CLASSICS.
Illustrated®

Emily Brontë
WUTHERING HEIGHTS

essay by
Abigail Burnham Bloom, Ph.D.

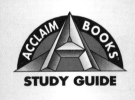

STUDY GUIDE

Wuthering Heights
Originally published as Classics Illustrated no. 59

Art by Henry Kiefer
Adaption by H. Miller
Cover by Rebecca Guay

For Classics Illustrated Study Guides
computer recoloring by Twilight Graphics
editor: Madeleine Robins
assistant editor: Valerie D'Orazio
design: Joseph Caponsacco

Dale-Chall R.L.: 6.05

ISBN 1-57840-051-1

Acclaim Books, New York, NY
Printed in the United States

WUTHERING HEIGHTS

by EMILY BRONTË

CATHY

HEATHCLIFF

HINDLEY

EDGAR

LINTON

CATHERINE

ELLEN

WUTHERING HEIGHTS, AN OLD ENGLISH MANSION, WAS SITUATED ON TOP OF A BLEAK HILL NEAR THE ENGLISH COAST. HERE LIVED THE EARNSHAW FAMILY, CONSISTING OF MR. AND MRS. EARNSHAW AND THEIR TWO CHILDREN, HINDLEY AND CATHY. ONE NIGHT, WHILE WAITING UP FOR THE RETURN OF MR. EARNSHAW, WHO HAD BEEN ON A TRIP TO LIVERPOOL . . .

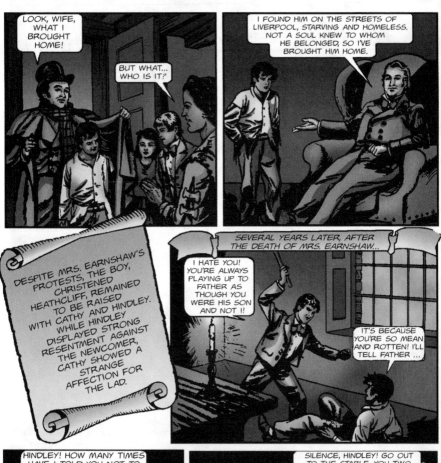

ALL WAS FAIRLY PEACEFUL AND QUIET FOR THE NEXT THREE YEARS. THEN MR EARNSHAW DIED AND HINDLEY CAME HOME TO THE FUNERAL . . . BRINGING A STRANGE WOMAN WITH HIM . . .

NELLY, MEET MY WIFE...WE'VE COME HOME TO STAY.

WIFE! WELL, WELCOME TO WUTHERING HEIGHTS.

YOU MUST WASH UP, MY DEAR, AND I'LL FIX UP A ROOM FOR YOU AND HINDLEY.

HINDLEY WAS NOW MASTER . . .

YOU AND JOSEPH MUST HENCEFORTH CONFINE YOURSELVES TO THE BACK KITCHEN AND LEAVE THE HOUSE TO ME!

AS FOR YOU, HEATHCLIFF, YOU'LL LIVE WITH THE SERVANTS AND WILL RECEIVE NO INSTRUCTION FROM THE CURATE!

IT IS MY WISH THAT YOU SPEND YOUR TIME OUTDOORS LABORING WITH THE OTHER HELP ON THE FARM. I SHALL BE THE MASTER OF WUTHERING HEIGHTS!

HEATHCLIFF BORE HIS DEGRADATION WELL. CATHY TAUGHT HIM WHAT SHE LEARNED AND WORKED OR PLAYED WITH HIM IN THE FIELDS . . .

IMAGINE THEM QUARRELING OVER A HEAP OF WARM HAIR!

YOU'D THINK THEY'D BE HAPPY LIVING IN SUCH A LOVELY HOUSE, WITH ALL THOSE PRETTY CLOTHES AND EVERYTHING!

HEARING THE INTRUDERS OUTSIDE THE WINDOW ...

THERE'S SOMEBODY OUTSIDE THE WINDOW!

OH, MAMA, MAMA! OH! PAPA ... COME HERE, QUICK!

AS CATHY AND HEATHCLIFF STARTED TO RUN AWAY, THEY WERE ATTACKED BY A SAVAGE DOG.

RUN, HEATHCLIFF, RUN! BEFORE THE DOG GETS YOU, TOO!

LET GO, YOU CURSED BEAST!

KEEP FAST, SKULKER! KEEP ... GOOD HEAVENS, IT'S A LITTLE GIRL!

THE DOG WAS BEATEN OFF AND THE SERVANT CARRIED CATHY INTO THE HOUSE ...

WHAT PREY, ROBERT?

SKULKER HAS CAUGHT A LITTLE GIRL, SIR ... AND THERE'S A LAD HERE, TOO!

SHAKE HANDS, HEATHCLIFF...ONCE, IN A WAY THAT IS PERMITTED!

I SHALL NOT! I SHALL NOT STAND TO BE LAUGHED AT...I SHALL NOT BEAR IT!

I DID NOT MEAN TO LAUGH AT YOU, HEATHCLIFF! IT WAS ONLY THAT YOU LOOKED ODD...AND YOU ARE SO DIRTY!

I SHALL BE DIRTY AS I PLEASE...AND I LIKE TO BE DIRTY!

WITH THAT, HE DASHED OUT OF THE ROOM, AMID THE MERRIMENT OF THE MASTER AND MISTRESS AND TO THE SERIOUS DISTURBANCE OF CATHY...

CHRISTMAS EVE CAME. THE EARNSHAWS MADE PREPERATIONS TO RECEIVE EDGAR AND ISABELLA LINTON, WHO HAD BEEN INVITED FOR THE MORROW...

CHRISTMAS MORNING...

NELLY, MAKE ME DECENT WHILE THE OTHERS ARE IN CHURCH!

WELL, IT IS CERTAINLY HIGH TIME, HEATHCLIFF!

THEIR CONVERSATION WAS INTERRUPTED BY A RAMBLING SOUND MOVING UP THE ROAD AND ENTERING THE COURT...

THERE ARE THE LINTONS, NOW! YOU MUST BE ON YOUR BEST BEHAVIOR AND GREET THEM PLEASANTLY.

AS HEATHCLIFF OPENED THE DOOR LEADING FROM THE KITCHEN...

JOSEPH, KEEP THE FELLOW OUT OF THE PARLOR...SEND HIM TO THE GARRET TILL DINNER IS OVER. HE'LL BE CRAMMING HIS FINGERS INTO EVERYTHING IF LET ALONE A MINUTE.

NAY, SIR, HE'LL TOUCH NOTHING, NOT HE... AND I SUPPOSE HE MUST HAVE HIS SHARE OF THE DAINTIES AS WELL AS WE.

HE SHALL HAVE HIS SHARE OF MY HANDS! I'LL PULL THOSE ELEGANT LOCKS OF HIS A BIT LONGER!

THEY'RE LONG ENOUGH ALREADY! I WONDER WHY THEY DON'T MAKE HIS HEAD ACHE.

WILD WITH RAGE, HEATHCLIFF SEIZED A TUREEN OF HOT APPLESAUCE AND HURLED IT AT EDGAR, HIS TORMENTOR...

THAT'LL TEACH YOU TO HOLD YOUR TONGUE!

IN THE EVENING, A BAND OF MUSICIANS ARRIVED AND THE ROOM WAS CLEARED FOR DANCING. AFTER A WHILE, CAROLS WERE SUNG. AT THE HEIGHT OF THE SINGING, CATHY QUIETLY STOLE OUT OF THE ROOM . . .

ELLEN FOLLOWED HER UP TO THE GARRET

SHE'S GONE TO HEATHCLIFF'S ROOM. I KNEW SHE COULDN'T FORGET HER FORMER PLAYMATE!

A MOMENT LATER, ELLEN REACHED THE GARRET DOOR . . .

GOOD HEAVENS, SHE MUST HAVE CLIMBED INTO THE ROOM THROUGH THE SKYLIGHT.

THERE WAS NO REPONSE FROM WITHIN . . .

HEATHCLIFF! PLEASE OPEN UP . . . I WISH TO SPEAK TO YOU.

SOON THEY CAME OUT OF THE ROOM BY WAY OF THE SKYLIGHT. ELLEN TOOK HEATHCLIFF DOWN TO THE KITCHEN WHILE CATHY WENT BACK TO THE PARTY . . .

WHAT ARE YOU THINKING ABOUT, HEATHCLIFF?

I'M TRYING TO SETTLE HOW I SHALL PAY HINDLEY BACK.

FOR SHAME! IT IS FOR GOD TO PUNISH WICKED PEOPLE . . . WE SHOULD LEARN TO FORGIVE.

NO, GOD WON'T HAVE THE SATISFACTION THAT I SHALL!

IN DUE COURSE, A CHILD WAS BORN TO THE EARNSHAWS, BUT THE MOTHER DIED SOON AFTER. OVERCOME BY HIS GRIEF, HINDLEY GAVE HIMSELF UP TO RECKLESS DISSIPATION.

THE CHILD, HARETON, BECAME THE PARTICULAR CHARGE OF ELLEN DEAN . . .

IT LOOKS LIKE I'LL HAVE TO BE MOTHER AND FATHER TO YOU FROM NOW ON, MY LITTLE SWEET!

SOMETIME LATER, WHILE HINDLEY WAS AWAY FROM THE HEIGHTS . . .

CATHY, ARE YOU BUSY THIS AFTERNOON? ARE YOU GOING OUT?

NO, IT IS RAINING, HEATHCLIFF.

WHY HAVE YOU THAT SILK FROCK ON, THEN? NOBODY COMING HERE, I HOPE!

NOT THAT I KNOW OF...BUT YOU SHOULD BE IN THE FIELD NOW, HEATHCLIFF. IT IS AN HOUR PAST DINNER-TIME...YOU SHOULD BE GONE!

HINDLEY DOES NOT OFTEN FREE US FROM HIS ACCURSED PRESENCE! I'LL STAY WITH YOU! YOU'VE BEEN MORE WITH THE LINTONS THAN WITH ME!

THEIR CONVERSATION WAS INTERRUPTED BY THE SOUND OF A HORSE'S HOOFS IN THE COURT...

EDGAR LINTON SOON CAME IN AND CATHY MARKED THE DIFFERENCE BETWEEN HER FRIENDS... AS ONE CAME IN, AND THE OTHER LEFT...

SO SHE WAS EXPECTING COMPANY!

I'M NOT COME TOO SOON, AM I?

NO. WHAT ARE YOU DOING THERE, NELLY?

HINDLEY HAD GIVEN ELLEN INSTRUCTIONS TO BE PRESENT AT ANY PRIVATE VISITS OF EDGAR LINTON...

MY WORK, MISS!

SHE STEPPED BEHIND ELLEN AND WHISPERED CROSSLY...

TAKE YOURSELF AND YOUR DUSTER OFF! WHEN COMPANY IS IN THE HOUSE, SERVANTS DON'T COMMENCE CLEANING N THE ROOM WHERE THEY ARE!

I'M SURE MR. LINTON WILL EXCUSE ME!

IRRESISTIBLY IMPELLED BY THE MEAN SPIRIT WITHIN HER, CATHY SLAPPED HER ON THE CHEEK...

CATHERINE, LOVE! CATHERINE!

INSTEAD OF LEAVING THE HOUSE, HEATHCLIFF FLUNG HIMSELF ON A BENCH NEAR THE WALL IN THE KITCHEN . . .

SOME TIME LATER, CATHY, UNAWARE OF HEATHCLIFF'S PRESENCE . . .

ARE YOU ALONE, NELLY? WHERE'S HEATHCLIFF?

ABOUT HIS WORK IN THE STABLE, I SUPPOSE!

EDGAR LINTON ASKED ME TO MARRY HIM. NOW, BEFORE I TELL YOU WHAT MY ANSWER WAS, YOU TELL ME WHAT IT OUGHT TO HAVE BEEN!

I MUST SAY HE IS HOPELESSLY STUPID OR A VENTURE-SOME FOOL. WHAT ABOUT HEATHCLIFF?

IT WOULD DEGRADE ME TO MARRY HEATHCLIFF NOW . . . SO HE SHALL NEVER KNOW HOW I LOVE HIM. WHATEVER OUR SOULS ARE MADE OF, THEY'RE THE SAME!

HEATHCLIFF HAD LISTENED TILL HE HEARD CATHY SAY HE WOULD DEGRADE HER, AND THEN STOLE NOISELESSLY OUT . . .

CATHY, I'VE COME TO THE CONCLUSION THAT YOU ARE A WICKED, UNPRINCIPLED GIRL! IF YOU MARRY EDGAR, YOU'LL REGRET IT AS LONG AS YOU LIVE!

HEATHCLIFF HAD COMPLETELY DISAPPEARED FROM WUTHERING HEIGHTS. SOME TIME LATER, CATHY AND EDGAR LINTON WERE MARRIED . . .

SOON AFTER THEIR MARRIAGE . . .

NELLY, I WANT YOU TO COME AND LIVE WITH ME AT THRUSHCROSS GRANGE.

NO, CATHERINE, I MUST STAY HERE WITH HARETON!

WHEN ELLEN REFUSED, CATHY PREVAILED UPON HER HUSBAND AND BROTHER HINDLEY TO PERSUADE HER TO LEAVE WUTHERING HEIGHTS . . .

I'LL HAVE NO MORE OF THIS, ELLEN! PACK UP AND GO! I WANT NO WOMAN IN THE HOUSE, NOW THAT THERE'S NO MISTRESS. THE CURATE WILL TAKE THE CHILD IN HAND LATER!

I'LL GO, MASTER HINDLEY, BUT I MUST SAY YOU GOT RID OF ALL DECENT PEOPLE ONLY TO RUN TO RUIN A LITTLE FASTER.

ELLEN HAD NO OTHER CHOICE BUT TO OBEY HINDLEY'S ORDERS. AND SO, MUCH AGAINST HER WISHES, SHE TEARFULLY SAID GOODBYE TO HARETON AND LEFT WUTHERING HEIGHTS . . .

EDGAR AND CATHY LIVED HAPPILY AT THRUSHCROSS GRANGE FOR THE NEXT SIX MONTHS, EACH SHOWING THE UTMOST RESPECT FOR, AND DEVOTION TO, THE OTHER. THEN, ON A MELLOW EVENING IN SEPTEMBER, CAME A BREAK IN THEIR PLACID EXISTENCE . . .

ELLEN WAS COMING FROM THE GARDEN WITH A HEAVY BASKET OF APPLES SHE HAD BEEN GATHERING . . .

SUDDENLY, AS SHE STOPPED TO REST BY THE KITCHEN DOOR . . .

I HAVE WAITED HERE AN HOUR . . . I DARED NOT ENTER! LOOK, I'M NOT A STRANGER!

WHAT! YOU COME BACK? IS IT REALLY . .

YES, HEATHCLIFF! ARE THEY AT HOME . . . WHERE IS SHE? I MUST HAVE ONE WORD WITH YOUR MISTRESS! TELL HER SOME PERSON FROM GIMMERTON DESIRES TO SEE HER!

HOW WILL SHE TAKE IT? IT WILL PUT HER OUT OF HER HEAD . . . AND, YOU ARE HEATHCLIFF, BUT ALTERED. I HARDLY RECOGNIZED YOU.

GO AND CARRY MY MESSAGE. I CANNOT REST TILL YOU DO.

ELLEN SOON ENTERED THE PARLOUR...

A PERSON FROM GIMMERTON WISHES TO SEE YOU, MA'AM.

WISHES TO SEE ME? WELL, CLOSE THE CURTAINS, NELLY, AND BRING UP TEA! I'LL BE BACK DIRECTLY!

A MOMENT LATER...

OH, EDGAR, EDGAR!

OH, EDGAR, DARLING... HEATHCLIFF'S COME BACK... HE IS!

WELL, WELL, DON'T STRANGLE ME FOR THAT! HE NEVER STRUCK ME AS A MARVELOUS TREASURE. THERE IS NO NEED TO BE FRANTIC.

I KNOW YOU DIDN'T LIKE HIM, YET FOR MY SAKE YOU MUST BE FRIENDS NOW! SHALL I TELL HIM TO COME UP?

ELLEN WILL FETCH HIM... AND CATHERINE, TRY TO BE GLAD WITHOUT BEING ABSURD. THE WHOLE HOUSEHOLD NEED NOT WITNESS THE SIGHT OF YOUR WELCOMING A RUNAWAY SERVANT AS A BROTHER.

A FEW MOMENTS LATER, AFTER AN AWKWARD EXCHANGE OF GREETINGS...

SIT DOWN, SIR. OF COURSE, I AM HAPPY TO SEE YOU... IF IT PLEASES MRS. LINTON.

CRUEL HEATHCLIFF, YOU DO NOT DESERVE THIS WELCOME. TO BE ABSENT AND SILENT FOR SO LONG, AND NEVER TO THINK OF ME!

A LITTLE MORE THAN YOU HAVE THOUGHT OF ME. I'VE FOUGHT THROUGH A BITTER LIFE SINCE I LAST HEARD YOUR VOICE.

CATHERINE, UNLESS WE ARE TO HAVE COLD TEA, PLEASE COME UP TO THE TABLE. MR. HEATHCLIFF WILL HAVE A LONG WALK WHEREVER HE MAY LODGE TONIGHT, AND I'M THIRSTY!

AN HOUR LATER . . .

ARE YOU GOING TO GIMMERTON?

NO, TO WUTHERING HEIGHTS. MR. EARNSHAW INVITED ME WHEN I CALLED THIS MORNING.

WHEN HEATHCLIFF LEFT, ELLEN PONDERED HIS LAST WORDS PAINFULLY . . .

MR. EARNSHAW INVITED HIM . . . AND HE CALLED ON MR. EARNSHAW! I FEAR HE'S COME BACK TO WORK SOME MISCHIEF! WHY DID HE HAVE TO COME BACK?

IN THE DAYS THAT FOLLOWED, HEATHCLIFF WAS A FREQUENT VISITOR TO THE LINTONS. ISABELLA LINTON, NOW A CHARMING YOUNG LADY OF EIGHTEEN, SUDDENLY SHOWED AN IRRESISTIBLE ATTRACTION TOWARD THE TOLERATED GUEST . . .

SHE GREW CROSS AND IRRITABLE WITH THE OTHER MEMBERS OF THE HOUSEHOLD. ONE EVENING . . .

IT'S YOUR HARSHNESS THAT MAKES ME UNHAPPY!

HOW CAN YOU SAY I AM HARSH? WHEN HAVE I BEEN HARSH?

YESTERDAY, IN OUR WALK ALONG THE MOOR! YOU TOLD ME TO RAMBLE WHERE I PLEASED, WHILE YOU SAUNTERED ON WITH MR. HEATHCLIFF!

AND THAT'S YOUR NOTION OF HARSHNESS? WHY YOU SILLY CHILD . . . I MERELY THOUGHT THAT MR. HEATHCLIFF'S TALK WOULD HAVE NOTHING ENTERTAINING FOR YOUR EARS.

ISABELLA THEN CRIED OUT . . .

I LOVE HIM MORE THAN YOU EVER LOVED EDGAR! AND HE MIGHT LOVE ME IF YOU WOULD LET HIM!

I WOULDN'T BE YOU FOR A KINGDOM, THEN! YOU DON'T KNOW HEATHCLIFF LIKE I DO . . . HE IS A FIERCE, WOLFISH MAN! HE'D BE QUITE CAPABLE OF MARRYING YOU FOR YOUR FORTUNE AND EXPECTATIONS!

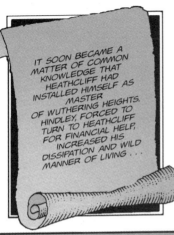

IT SOON BECAME A MATTER OF COMMON KNOWLEDGE THAT HEATHCLIFF HAD INSTALLED HIMSELF AS MASTER OF WUTHERING HEIGHTS. HINDLEY, FORCED TO TURN TO HEATHCLIFF FOR FINANCIAL HELP, INCREASED HIS DISSIPATION AND WILD MANNER OF LIVING . . .

ONE DAY, DEEPLY DISTURBED BY WHAT SHE HAD HEARD, ELLEN DECIDED TO PAY A VISIT TO WUTHERING HEIGHTS . . .

GOD BLESS YOU, DARLING! HARETON, IT'S NELLY, YOUR NURSE!

HE RETREATED AND PICKED UP A LARGE STONE, CURSING AND SWEARING AS HE DID . . .

HE DOESN'T RECOGNIZE ME.

SHE OFFERED HIM AN ORANGE AND HE QUICKLY SNATCHED IT FROM HER HAND . . .

SHE OFFERED A SECOND ONE . . .

WHO HAS TAUGHT YOU THOSE FINE WORDS? THE CURATE?

BLAST THE CURATE AND YOU! GIVE ME THAT!

YOUR WORTHLESS FRIEND, THE SNEAKING RASCAL YONDER! AH, HE'S CAUGHT A GLIMPSE OF US... HE'S COMING IN! I WONDER WILL HE HAVE THE HEART TO FIND A PLAUSIBLE EXCUSE FOR MAKING LOVE TO MISS!

A MOMENT LATER, HEATHCLIFF OPENED THE DOOR...

HEATHCLIFF, WHAT ARE YOU ABOUT, RAISING THIS STIR? I SAID YOU MUST LET ISABELLA ALONE! DO YOU WANT EDGAR TO FORBID YOUR COMING HERE?

HE'D BETTER NOT TRY! I'VE A RIGHT TO KISS HER, IF SHE CHOOSES, AND YOU'VE NO RIGHT TO OBJECT! I'M NOT YOUR HUSBAND... YOU NEEDN'T BE JEALOUS OF ME!

IF YOU LIKE ISABELLA, YOU SHALL MARRY HER... BUT I KNOW YOU DON'T LIKE HER! ON THE CONTRARY, YOU TOLD ME YOURSELF YOU HATED HER!

I HAVE MY OWN GOOD REASONS FOR WHAT I DO, CATHY! IF I IMAGINED YOU REALLY WANTED ME TO MARRY HER, I'D CUT MY THROAT!

ELLEN LEFT THEM TO SEEK EDGAR, WHO WAS WONDERING WHAT KEPT CATHY BELOW SO LONG...

ELLEN, HAVE YOU SEEN YOUR MISTRESS?

YES, SHE'S IN THE KITCHEN. SHE'S SADLY PUT OUT BY MR. HEATHCLIFF'S BEHAVIOR, AND, INDEED, I THINK IT TIME TO CALL OFF HIS VISITS HERE.

ELLEN THEN RELATED WHAT HAD HAPPENED . . .

THIS IS INSUFFERABLE! CALL ME TWO MEN OUT OF THE HALL, ELLEN. I HAVE HUMORED CATHERINE AND HER FRIEND ENOUGH!

A MOMENT LATER . . .

YOUR PRESENCE, SIR, IS A MORAL POISON, AND I GIVE YOU THREE MINUTES TO LEAVE THIS HOUSE, NEVER TO RETURN!

CATHY, THIS LAMB OF YOURS THREATENS LIKE A BULL! IT IS IN DANGER OF SPLITTING ITS SKULL AGAINST MY KNUCKLES!

AS HEATHCLIFF APPROACHED IN A THREATENING MANNER, EDGAR SPRANG AT HIM AND STRUCK HIM FULL ON THE THROAT AND RAN OUT OF THE ROOM . . .

YOU MUST LEAVE, HEATHCLIFF! HE'LL RETURN WITH A BRACE OF PISTOLS AND HALF A DOZEN MEN!

I'LL CRUSH HIS RIBS LIKE A ROTTEN HAZEL-NUT BEFORE I CROSS THE THRESHOLD! LET ME GET AT HIM!

EDGAR RETURNED WITH SOME OF THE MEN SERVANTS AND HEATHCLIFF WAS FORCED TO LEAVE . . .

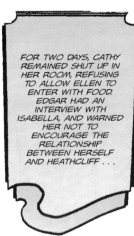

FOR TWO DAYS, CATHY REMAINED SHUT UP IN HER ROOM, REFUSING TO ALLOW ELLEN TO ENTER WITH FOOD. EDGAR HAD AN INTERVIEW WITH ISABELLA, AND WARNED HER NOT TO ENCOURAGE THE RELATIONSHIP BETWEEN HERSELF AND HEATHCLIFF . . .

ON THE THIRD DAY, CATHY OPENED THE DOOR TO ELLEN . . .

IT'S ABOUT TIME YOU CAME TO YOUR SENSES, MISS. I'D THINK YOU'D SHOW SOME CONSIDERATION FOR MR. LINTON, AT LEAST!

WHAT IS THAT APATHETIC THING DOING? HAS HE FALLEN INTO A TRANCE OR IS HE DEAD?

HE'S TOLERABLY WELL, I THINK! HE'S CONTINUALLY AMONG HIS BOOKS, SINCE HE HAS NO OTHER SOCIETY.

AMONG HIS BOOKS! AND HERE I AM DYING! IS HE ACTUALLY SO INDIFFERENT TO MY LIFE?

WHY, MA'AM, THE MASTER HAS NO IDEA YOU'RE IN DANGER! SURELY, HE DOESN'T FEAR THAT YOU'LL LET YOURSELF DIE OF HUNGER!

HOWEVER, CONTRARY TO ELLEN'S BELIEF, CATHY WAS DESPERATELY ILL. SHE WAS IN GRAVE DANGER OF LOSING HER MIND. THE COUNTY DOCTOR WAS CALLED AND KEPT WATCH OVER HER ALL THAT NIGHT . . .

SHE HAS PASSED THE CRISIS. BUT I WARN YOU TO KEEP HER FREE FROM ANY EXCITEMENT, OR I CANNOT BE RESPONSIBLE FOR THE CONSEQUENCES.

HOW IS SHE, DOCTOR?

OH, MASTER, MASTER, OUR YOUNG LADY, ISABELLA . . .

HUSH, MARY, WHAT IS THE MATTER? WHAT AILS YOUR YOUNG LADY?

SHE'S GONE, SHE'S GONE! HEATHCLIFF'S RUN OFF WITH HER!

THAT'S NOT TRUE! HOW HAS THE IDEA ENTERED YOUR HEAD? ELLEN, GO AND SEEK HER.

ELLEN RETURNED, CONFIRMING THE SERVANT'S STATEMENT . . .

ARE WE TO TRY ANY MEASURES FOR OVERTAKING HER AND BRINGING HER BACK? HOW SHOULD WE DO?

SHE WENT OF HER OWN ACCORD. TROUBLE ME NO MORE ABOUT HER . . . HEREAFTER, SHE'S MY SISTER IN NAME ONLY.

ISABELLA LIVED AT WUTHERING HEIGHTS, WHERE SHE WAS CRUELLY MISTREATED BY HEATHCLIFF.

ONE DAY, WHILE EDGAR WAS ABSENT, HEATHCLIFF PAID A SECRET VISIT TO CATHY AT THRUSHCROSS GRANGE. THE EXCITEMENT WAS TOO MUCH FOR HER AND AT MIDNIGHT OF THE SAME DAY, SHE DIED, AFTER GIVING BIRTH TO A DAUGHTER . . .

POOR EDGAR . . . BUT HIS SORROW IS NOTHING TO THAT OF HEATHCLIFF'S WHEN HE LEARNS OF CATHY'S DEATH.

HEATHCLIFF, WHO HAD PROMISED TO RETURN THE NEXT DAY, WAS ACCOSTED BY ELLEN IN THE GARDEN, BEFORE SHE COULD SAY ANYTHING . . .

SHE'S DEAD! I'VE NOT WAITED FOR YOU, TO LEARN THAT! DON'T SNIVEL BEFORE ME . . . SHE WANTS NONE OF YOUR TEARS!

YES, SHE'S DEAD! GONE TO HEAVEN, I HOPE, WHERE WE MAY ALL JOIN HER IF WE TAKE DUE WARNING AND LEAVE OUR EVIL WAYS TO FIND GOOD!

HOW DID SHE DIE? DID SHE EVER MENTION ME?

QUIETLY AS A LAMB. HER LIFE CLOSED IN A GENTLE DREAM.

AT THAT, HE CRIED OUT IN ANGUISH . . .

CATHERINE EARNSHAW, MAY YOU NOT REST AS LONG AS I AM LIVING! BE WITH ME ALWAYS . . . TAKE MY FORM . . . DRIVE ME MAD! DON'T LEAVE ME IN THE ABYSS WHERE I CANNOT FIND YOU! I CANNOT LIVE WITHOUT MY LIFE! I CANNOT LIVE WITHOUT MY SOUL!

HEATHCLIFF RETURNED TO WUTHERING HEIGHTS. AT THE FUNERAL THE ONLY MOURNERS WERE LINTON AND THE SERVANTS. THE DAY AFTER THE FUNERAL, LINTON KEPT TO HIS ROOM WHILE THE PARLOR WAS CONVERTED INTO A NURSERY FOR HIS CHILD, WHO WAS NAMED CATHERINE . . .

THAT SAME AFTERNOON, ISABELLA ENTERED THE PARLOR LAUGHING GIDDILY. THINKING IT WAS A SERVANT, ELLEN CALLED OUT . . .

HAVE DONE! HOW DARE YOU SHOW YOUR GIDDINESS HERE? WHAT WOULD MR. LINTON SAY IF HE HEARD YOU?

A FAMILIAR VOICE ANSWERED . . .

EXCUSE ME, BUT I KNOW EDGAR IS IN BED AND I CANNOT HELP MYSELF!

I HAVE RUN THE WHOLE WAY FROM WUTHERING HEIGHTS! THERE SHALL BE AN EXPLANATION AS SOON AS I CAN GIVE IT! ONLY JUST HAVE THE GOODNESS TO ORDER THE CARRIAGE TO TAKE ME TO GIMMERTON.

MRS. HEATH-CLIFF!

I SHALL HEAR NOTHING TILL YOU HAVE CHANGED INTO FRESH CLOTHES! CERTAINLY YOU SHALL NOT GO TO GIMMERTON TONIGHT!

ISABELLA TOLD ELLEN OF HER ESCAPE FROM HEATHCLIFF . . .

AH, HE WAS IN SUCH A FURY, HE'D BE CAPABLE OF COMING HERE TO SEE ME, TO TEASE EDGAR. I DARE NOT STAY LEST THAT NOTION POSSESS HIS WICKED HEAD!

ISABELLA THEN WENT INTO A LONG RECITAL OF HER TERRIFYING EXPERIENCES AT WUTHERING HEIGHTS. AN HOUR LATER, SHE LEFT . . . NEVER TO RETURN.

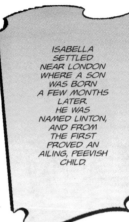

ISABELLA SETTLED NEAR LONDON WHERE A SON WAS BORN A FEW MONTHS LATER. HE WAS NAMED LINTON, AND FROM THE FIRST PROVED AN AILING, PEEVISH CHILD.

HEATHCLIFF DISCOVERED ISABELLA'S RESIDENCE AND THE EXISTENCE OF THE CHILD, BUT CHOSE NOT TO MOLEST THEM FOR THE MOMENT. BUT LATER . . .

SO THEY NAMED HIM LINTON . . . THEY WISH ME TO HATE IT, TOO, DO THEY?

I DON'T THINK THEY WISH YOU TO KNOW ANYTHING ABOUT IT!

BUT I'LL HAVE IT WHEN I WANT IT. THEY MAY RECKON ON THAT!

HINDLEY EARNSHAW DIED SOON AFTER, AND ELLEN WENT TO ATTEND THE FUNERAL . . .

THAT FOOL'S BODY SHOULD BE BURIED AT THE CROSSROADS, WITHOUT CEREMONY OF ANY KIND!

HE SEIZED HARETON AND LIFTED HIM ON THE TABLE . . .

THEY'LL NOT TAKE YOU BACK, MY BONNY LAD . . . YOU ARE MINE! AND WE'LL SEE IF ONE TREE WON'T GROW AS CROOKED AS ANOTHER, WITH THE SAME WIND TO TWIST IT!

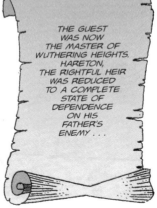

THE GUEST WAS NOW THE MASTER OF WUTHERING HEIGHTS. HARETON, THE RIGHTFUL HEIR WAS REDUCED TO A COMPLETE STATE OF DEPENDENCE ON HIS FATHER'S ENEMY . . .

PEACE AND HAPPINESS MARKED THE NEXT TWELVE YEARS AT THRUSHCROSS GRANGE. DISTURBED ONE DAY BY THE NEWS ISABELLA HEATHCLIFF WAS DYING, EDGAR LEFT TO BE WITH HIS SISTER, LEAVING ELLEN ALONE WITH CATHY, NOW A YOUNG LADY, AND THE SERVANTS . . .

A FEW DAYS LATER, EDGAR RETURNED, ACCOMPANIED BY LINTON, ISABELLA'S SON . . .

THIS IS YOUR COUSIN CATHERINE, LINTON! SHE'S FOND OF YOU ALREADY! AND MIND YOU, DON'T GRIEVE HER BY CRYING TONIGHT!

LET ME GO TO BED, THEN; I'M SO TIRED!

OH, HE'LL DO VERY WELL . . . VERY WELL, IF WE CAN KEEP HIM!

AY, IF WE CAN KEEP HIM.

SEVERAL HOURS LATER, ELLEN'S WORST FEARS WERE REALIZED . . .

WHAT BRINGS YOU FROM YOUR MASTER'S HOUSE, JOSEPH?

HEATHCLIFF HAS SENT ME FOR HIS LAD, AND I MAY NOT GO BACK WITHOUT HIM.

KNOWING IT WOULD BE USELESS TO KEEP LINTON AWAY FROM HIS RIGHTFUL FATHER, EDGAR RELUCTANTLY PROMISED TO SEND HIM OVER THE NEXT MORNING . . .

NEXT MORNING, HEATHCLIFF TOOK POSSESSION OF HIS RIGHTFUL HEIR...

I HOPE YOU'LL BE KIND TO THE BOY, HEATHCLIFF... OR YOU'LL NOT KEEP HIM LONG! AND REMEMBER, HE IS THE ONLY KIN YOU HAVE LEFT IN THE WORLD.

I'LL BE VERY KIND TO HIM, YOU NEEDN'T FEAR!

YES, NELL, MY SON IS PROSPECTIVE OWNER OF YOUR PLACE AND I SHOULD NOT WISH HIM TO DIE TILL I WAS CERTAIN OF BEING HIS SUCCESSOR! I DESPISE HIM FOR HIMSELF, AND I AM BITTERLY DISAPPOINTED WITH THE WHINING LITTLE WRETCH!

TIME WORE ON AT THE GRANGE IN A PLEASANT WAY TILL CATHERINE WAS SIXTEEN. ONE MORNING, SHE AND ELLEN DECIDED TO TAKE A RAMBLE ON THE EDGE OF THE MOORS...

WAIT FOR ME, CATHY, YOU'LL GET LOST!

WE'RE GETTING DANGEROUSLY CLOSE TO HEATHCLIFF'S PROPERTY, AND MR. LINTON HAS WARNED ME TO KEEP HER AWAY FROM THERE!

A MOMENT LATER...

WHAT ARE YOU DOING POACHING ON MY PROPERTY? AFTER GROUSE EGGS, I SUPPOSE?

I'VE NEITHER TAKEN NOR FOUND ANY! PAPA TOLD ME THERE WERE QUANTITIES OF EGGS HERE, AND I WISHED TO SEE THEM!

AND WHO IS PAPA?

MR. LINTON, OF THRUSHCROSS GRANGE! I THOUGHT YOU DIDN'T KNOW ME OR YOU WOULD NOT HAVE SPOKEN THAT WAY! IS THAT YOUR SON?

NO, HE IS NOT MY SON, BUT I HAVE ONE AND I WOULD LIKE YOU TO MEET HIM.

MISS CATHERINE, WE REALLY MUST GO BACK!

CATHERINE INSISTED ON ENTERING THE HOUSE, DESPITE ELLEN'S OBJECTIONS . . .

YOU DON'T REMEMBER HIM? THAT'S LINTON, YOUR COUSIN YOU ALWAYS WISHED SO MUCH TO SEE!

IS THAT LITTLE LINTON? HE'S TALLER THAN I AM. ARE YOU LINTON?

THE YOUTH STEPPED FORWARD AND CATHERINE KISSED HIM FERVENTLY . . .

AND YOU ARE MY UNCLE, THEN. I THOUGHT I LIKED YOU, THOUGH YOU WERE CROSS AT FIRST. WHY DON'T YOU VISIT AT THE GRANGE WITH LINTON?

THERE, HANG IT! IF YOU HAVE ANY KISSES TO SPARE, GIVE THEM TO LINTON . . . THEY ARE THROWN AWAY ON ME!

I'D BETTER WARN YOU NOT TO TELL YOUR FATHER OF YOUR VISIT HERE, OR HE WILL FORBID YOUR COMING HERE AGAIN! YOU SEE, WE QUARRELED AT ONE TIME.

IT WAS SEVERAL MONTHS LATER BEFORE CATHERINE COULD PERSUADE ELLEN TO TAKE HER THERE AGAIN . . .

NO, NO, DON'T KISS ME, MISS LINTON . . . IT TAKES MY BREATH AWAY!

I HEAR YOU ARE ILL . . . CAN I DO YOU ANY GOOD?

WHY DIDN'T YOU COME BEFORE? DO YOU KNOW THAT BRUTE HARETON LAUGHS AT ME? I HATE HIM . . . INDEED I HATE THEM ALL . . . THEY ARE ODIOUS BEINGS!

ABOUT THIS TIME, EDGAR LINTON BECAME VERY ILL AND WAS CONFINED TO HIS ROOM MOST OF THE TIME. CATHY CONTINUED HER SECRET VISITS TO WUTHERING HEIGHTS AND WAS SLOWLY FALLING INTO THE TRAP THAT HEATHCLIFF HAD SET FOR HER . . . THE BAIT BEING HIS WEAKLING SON, LINTON . . .

ONE DAY . . .

WELL, WE HAVE VISITORS AGAIN! HOW'S EVERYTHING AT THE GRANGE?

LOWERING HIS VOICE, HE SPOKE TO ELLEN . . .

I HEAR THAT EDGAR LINTON IS ON HIS DEATHBED!

MY MASTER IS DYING. A SAD THING IT WILL BE FOR US ALL . . . BUT A BLESSING FOR HIM.

LINTON SEEMS DETERMINED TO UPSET MY PLANS. I'D THANK HIS UNCLE TO BE QUICK, AND GO BEFORE HIM! IS HE PRETTY LIVELY WITH MISS LINTON GENERALLY?

ELLEN WAS RELEASED AFTER BEING HELD CAPTIVE FOUR DAYS AND WENT DIRECTLY TO HER MASTER'S ROOM. SHE RELATED HER EXPERIENCE AT WUTHERING HEIGHTS . . .

MY POOR BABY! THAT MONSTER IS PLOTTING TO SECURE MY PERSONAL PROPERTY THROUGH HER MARRIAGE TO LINTON! YOU MUST SEND FOR MY ATTORNEY TO CHANGE MY WILL!

ELLEN LOST NO TIME IN CARRYING OUT HIS INSTRUCTIONS . . .

SEND FOR MR. GREEN, THE ATTORNEY, AT ONCE . . . AND A HALF DOZEN OF THE MEN TO BRING MISS CATHERINE BACK!

LATE THE SAME AFTERNOON . . .

ELLEN, ELLEN, IS PAPA STILL ALIVE?

CATHERINE, IS IT REALLY YOU?

A MOMENT LATER . . .

I . . . AM . . . GOING TO HER! AND YOU, DARLING CHILD . . . SHALL COME TO US . . .

EDGAR DIED PEACEFULLY IN CATHERINE'S ARMS, THWARTED IN HIS PLAN TO CHANGE THE WILL . . .

LATER . . .

I'M GLAD FATHER DIED WITHOUT LEARNING THAT I'M MARRIED TO THE SON OF HIS BITTEREST ENEMY.

THEN HE DID CARRY OUT HIS THREAT. THE MONSTER WILL NOW LAY CLAIM TO YOU AS HIS OWN AND FORCE YOU TO LIVE WITH HIM AT WUTHERING HEIGHTS!

I'M RESIGNED TO IT, NELLY. LINTON IS ALL I HAVE NOW.

THE FOLLOWING NIGHT . . .

I'D LIKE NOTHING BETTER THAN TO HAVE LINTON COME AND LIVE WITH US! I'D NEVER BE HAPPY LIVING HERE WITHOUT YOU!

NOTHING COULD PLEASE ME BETTER, ELLEN, BUT I'M AFRAID IT'S TOO MUCH TO HOPE FOR!

SUDDENLY . . .

THAT DEVIL HEATHCLIFF IS COMING IN THROUGH THE COURT. SHALL I FASTEN THE DOOR IN HIS FACE?

YOU SPEAK TO HIM, NELLY! I HAVE NO DESIRE TO SEE HIM.

STOP! NO MORE RUNNING AWAY! I'VE COME TO FETCH YOU HOME!

LINTON NEEDS YOU! HE WAKES AND SHRIEKS DURING THE NIGHT AND CALLS YOU TO PROTECT HIM FROM ME! HE'S YOUR CONCERN NOW!

WHY NOT LET CATHERINE CONTINUE HERE AND SEND MASTER LINTON TO HER? AS YOU HATE THEM BOTH, YOU WON'T MISS THEM.

I'M SEEKING A TENANT FOR THE GRANGE. MAKE HASTE . . . AND DON'T OBLIGE ME TO COMPEL YOU!

THEY LEFT, LEAVING ELLEN TO CARE FOR THRUSHCROSS GRANGE . . .

UPON HER ARRIVAL AT THE HEIGHTS, CATHERINE WENT DIRECTLY TO LINTON'S ROOM. A MOMENT LATER, SHE CAME RUNNING DOWN THE STAIRS, CRYING FRANTICALLY...

LINTON IS VERY ILL, HEATHCLIFF... YOU MUST SEND FOR THE DOCTOR AT ONCE!

WE KNOW THAT! BUT HIS LIFE ISN'T WORTH A FARTHING, AND I WON'T SPEND A FARTHING ON HIM!

CATHERINE SPENT THE NEXT FEW DAYS NURSING HER DYING HUSBAND. THEN ONE NIGHT...

ZILLAH! TELL MR. HEATHCLIFF HIS SON IS DYING!

MERCY ME!

IN A FEW MINUTES, HE CAME INTO THE ROOM AND FOUND CATHERINE SEATED BY THE BED...

NOW, CATHERINE, HOW DO YOU FEEL?

HE'S SAFE, AND I'M FREE! I SHOULD FEEL WELL, BUT YOU'VE LEFT ME SO LONG TO STRUGGLE AGAINST DEATH ALONE, THAT I FEEL AND SEE ONLY DEATH!

SOME TIME LATER, ELLEN WAS SUMMONED TO WUTHERING HEIGHTS . . . AND OBEYED JOYFULLY FOR CATHERINE'S SAKE . . .

YOU SENT FOR ME?

YES, I'M TIRED OF CATHERINE. YOU'LL FIND HER IN THE KITCHEN!

NELLY! IT'S GOOD TO SEE YOU!

AND YOU, CATHY! YOU'RE LOOKING BADLY, MY CHILD!

CATHY POINTED TO HARETON . . .

NOT QUITE AS BADLY AS HE! LOOK, HE TWITCHES HIS NOSE LIKE MY DOG, JUNO, TWITCHES HERS.

MR. HARETON WILL TELL THE MASTER TO SEND YOU UPSTAIRS IF YOU DON'T BEHAVE!

DESPITE HER APPARENT CONTEMPT FOR HER COUSIN, CATHERINE REPEATEDLY MADE ATTEMPTS TO MAKE FRIENDS WITH HIM . . .

YOU SHOULD BE FRIENDS WITH CATHERINE, HARETON, SINCE SHE REPENTS HER SAUCINESS. IT WOULD MAKE YOU ANOTHER MAN TO HAVE HER FOR A COMPANION.

WHEN SHE HATES ME! NAY, I'D NOT SEEK HER GOODWILL IF IT WOULD MAKE ME KING!

IT IS NOT I WHO HATE YOU; IT IS YOU WHO HATE ME! YOU HATE ME EVEN MORE THAN MR. HEATHCLIFF!

WHY HAVE I ANGERED HIM, THEN, BY TAKING YOUR PART A HUNDRED TIMES? AND THAT, WHEN YOU DESPISED AND SNEERED AT ME?

I DIDN'T KNOW YOU TOOK MY PART, AND I WAS MISERABLE AND BITTER AT EVERYBODY . . . BUT NOW, I THANK YOU AND BEG YOUR FORGIVENESS.

CATHERINE BESTOWED A GENTLE KISS ON HIS CHEEK AND THEY WERE FAST FRIENDS THEREAFTER . . .

IT WAS ELLEN WHO FIRST NOTICED THE CHANGE THAT HAD COME OVER HEATHCLIFF IN THE NEXT FEW WEEKS. HE WOULD SPEND HIS NIGHTS AWAY FROM THE HOUSE AND AT HER CHANCE MEETINGS WITH HIM, SHE NOTICED A STRANGE AND JOYFUL LOOK IN HIS FACE THAT MADE HIM APPEAR EVEN EXUBERANT . . .

ONE MORNING . . .

WILL YOU HAVE SOME BREAKFAST? YOU MUST BE HUNGRY RAMBLING ABOUT ALL NIGHT.

NO, I'M NOT HUNGRY . . . JUST GO ABOUT YOUR WORK AND LET ME ALONE!

HE'LL WORK HIMSELF INTO A FIT OF ILLNESS! I CANNOT CONCEIVE WHAT HE HAS BEEN DOING!

HE LEFT HIS FOOD UNTOUCHED ALL DAY, AND THAT EVENING, ELLEN SPOKE TO HIM AGAIN . . .

HAVE YOU ANY GOOD NEWS, HEATHCLIFF? YOU LOOK UNCOMMONLY ANIMATED.

WHERE SHOULD GOOD NEWS COME FROM FOR ME? TODAY, I AM WITHIN SIGHT OF MY HEAVEN! I HAVE MY EYES WITHIN SIGHT OF IT!

AND NOW YOU'D BETTER GO! I CAN'T HAVE YOU PRYING INTO MY AFFAIRS!

IT RAINED ALL THAT NIGHT, AND NEXT MORNING, ELLEN CHANCED TO LOOK UP AT HEATHCLIFF'S WIDE-OPEN WINDOWS...

HE CANNOT BE IN BED... THOSE SHOWERS WOULD DRENCH HIM THROUGH! I'LL GO UP AND SEE FOR MYSELF!

ENTERING THE ROOM TO CLOSE THE WINDOWS, SHE RECEIVED A SEVERE SHOCK...

GOOD HEAVENS!

STARK DEAD!

SEIZED WITH A FIT OF TREMBLING, SHE CALLED OUT FOR JOSEPH...

JOSEPH, COME QUICKLY! THE MASTER'S DEAD!

JOSEPH SHUFFLED QUIETLY INTO THE ROOM...

THE DEVIL'S CARRIED OFF HIS SOUL, AND HE MAY HAVE HIS CARCASS INTO THE BARGAIN! WHAT A WICKED ONE HE LOOKS GRINNING AT DEATH!

HEATHCLIFF WAS BURIED IN ACCORDANCE WITH HIS WISHES, NEXT TO THE GRAVE OF CATHERINE EARNSHAW. CATHERINE LINTON AND HARETON WERE MARRIED AND WENT TO LIVE WITH ELLEN AT THRUSHCROSS GRANGE. JOSEPH WAS LEFT ALONE AT WUTHERING HEIGHTS, AND THE ROOMS WERE SHUT UP, LEFT FOR THE USE OF SUCH GHOSTS AS CHOSE TO INHABIT THEM...

THE END

WUTHERING HEIGHTS

EMILY BRONTE

This is a novel that has confounded the world since its publication in 1847. Its first reviewers thought it was coarse and incomprehensible, but it is now thought to be one of the very greatest novels in an era of great novels. Why this change? As readers, we have changed how we read novels, and *Wuthering Heights* helped us change; we enjoy novels that have an unusual vitality; we are more open to harsh subject matter, such as spousal abuse, child abuse, revenge, and kidnapping. In addition, we can now live with and accept this novel's ability to operate on both a spiritual and an earthly plane. For this is not a novel that has a simple meaning; its plot is as rich and complex as the poetic language the author uses.

about Emily from two main sources: the statements that her sister Charlotte made, and and Elizabeth Gaskell's biography of Charlotte, *The Life of Charlotte Brontë*, written in 1857.

Emily Jane Brontë was born on July 30, 1818, the fifth of six children: Maria, Elizabeth, Charlotte, Patrick Branwell, Emily, and Anne. In 1820, soon after her youngest sister, Anne, was born, the family moved to Haworth, a small town in Yorkshire, in northeast England. The Parsonage, which was to be their home for the rest of their lives, sits upon a hill. Surrounding the house on three sides is a graveyard, and behind are the moors where Emily was to spend so much of her time. The moors are not dramatic in the most romantic sense; rather, they are rugged, windy, and open. Emily's father was the perpetual curate (a position roughly on par with a vicar) at Haworth. He had raised himself from a humble beginning in Ireland to a university education and a career in the Church. After coming to live in Haworth, his wife soon succumbed to cancer and left her six children to be raised by her husband. When he could not persuade any other female acquaintance to marry him and mother his ready-made family, Patrick

THE AUTHOR

There are few tangible remains of Emily Brontë's astonishing creative talent. She left behind her remarkable poems, a few scraps of diary pages and letters, some drawings and paintings, and one great novel. It is not known whether Emily herself or someone else destroyed her early creative works and her letters. We know

Brontë was assisted by his wife's sister, called Aunt Branwell by the children. When she was six, Emily went with her three older sisters to Cowan Bridge, a school fictionalized by Charlotte as the Lowood School in *Jane Eyre*. It isn't known the extent to which Charlotte exaggerated the conditions of the school, but during their stay there the girls suffered from exposure to cold weather and a lack of good, healthy food. The two oldest girls, Maria and Elizabeth, were found to have consumption, and were brought back to Haworth where they soon died. Their father immediately sent for Charlotte and Emily to come home.

From this point onward the children were left much to their own. There were many books, magazines, and political discussions within the parsonage. They were used to exercising their active imaginations. Aunt Branwell gave the girls sewing lessons, they did work around the house, they practiced drawing, and they roamed over the moors. When their father bought Patrick Branwell (called Branwell) a box of toy soldiers, each of the four children chose a figure for his own, and they used these toy soldiers as the basis for intricate and involved stories. At first Emily was closest to her older sister, Charlotte, and they shared stories with each other. Then when Charlotte went to school again, Emily began to spend time with her younger sister, Anne. Together they invented the country of Gondal (Charlotte and Branwell invented another fantastic nation,

Angria). Still using the toy soldiers, they wrote books for their soldiers to read, and described the history, politics, and love affairs in their countries. These stories were written in microscopic handwriting, and bound into tiny volumes that the soldiers could hold in their hands.

Emily was tall and thin, her build athletic and her character strong and stoic. By nature extremely reserved, she was always happiest at home in Haworth. As a teenager she went away to school with Charlotte, but Emily was sent home with homesickness. Charlotte said of Emily, "Liberty was the breath of Emily's nostrils; without it, she perished." Whatever Emily's feelings in the matter, Mr. Brontë was not wealthy enough to support three unmarried daughters. The reality of their lives was that teaching, either at a school or as a governess, was the only profession open to them. Emily had a stint as a teacher at another school and was very unhappy there, so, hoping to earn a living closer to home, the sisters lit on the idea of running a school of their own in the parsonage. To further this plan Charlotte and Emily went to Brussels together in order to learn German and French. Their teacher stated later that he thought Emily's genius and logic and imagination were greater than Charlotte's. He wrote, "She should have been a man—a great navigator. Her powerful reason would have deduced new spheres of discovery from the knowledge of the old; and her strong, imperious will would never have been daunted by opposition or difficulty." After less than a year in Brussels the sisters were called back to Haworth when their aunt died. Charlotte went back to Brussels as a teacher, but Emily stayed at Haworth. She now had to take care of her father as well as her brother Branwell, who was destroying himself with alcohol and opium (and had disgraced himself with an unlucky love affair). Charlotte returned home after another year, and the sisters again thought of starting the school in their home. When no students could be found to attend their school, the sisters tried to find other ways of making money.

Charlotte Brontë told the story in her "Biographical Notice of Ellis and Acton Bell" of finding the manuscript of Emily's poetry. Despite the closeness of the sisters, Charlotte was unaware of how good Emily's poetry had become. She believed the poems unusual: "I thought them condensed and terse, vigorous and genuine. To my ear, they had also a peculiar music—wild, melancholy, and elevating." Charlotte had difficulty getting her sister Emily to accept the fact that she had read them, let alone that she wanted her to present them for the world to read. However, their third sister, Anne, had also been writing poetry, and together they published their slim volume, consisting of about twenty poems each, in 1846. They used the pseudonyms of Currer, Ellis, and Acton Bell, retaining their own initials but disguising their sex and identity, since writing was still considered an "unwomanly" pursuit. The volume was well reviewed in several places, but it sold only two copies.

Emily's poems show the life she led: a life in constant contact with death. She had more communion with her own imagination than with the outside world. Their house was surrounded by a graveyard, so that looking from her dining room window, Emily described the prospect:

The Case of the Missing Manuscript

Is it possible that Charlotte destroyed her sister's second novel? Consider the evidence. In 1847 Charlotte had completed her first novel, *The Professor*, Anne had completed *Agnes Gray,* and Emily had completed *Wuthering Heights*. During the next year Charlotte wrote *Jane Eyre* and Anne wrote *The Tenant of Wildfell Hall*. There is a reference in a letter to Emily from her publisher about a manuscript. It is not known if he is referring to *Wuthering Heights* or another novel. Charlotte was not a fan of *Wuthering Heights*. Charlotte revised the second edition of the novel for publication in 1850. In doing so she made many changes. Could Charlotte have destroyed Emily's second, and perhaps coarser, novel in order to protect her sister's reputation? We will probably never know.

I see around me tombstones grey
Stretching their shadows far
away.
Beneath the turf my footsteps
tread
Lie low and lone the silent dead

The Brontës were constantly aware of death through the death of those around them. Their father performed the services for village dead, and the bell in their church tolled to announce these deaths. Sometimes the verses, although written for one of her characters—usually an inhabitant of the imaginary kingdom of Gondal—seem to speak in Emily's voice. This is the first verse of the last poem that Emily is believed to have ever written:

No coward soul is mine
No trembler in the world's storm
troubled sphere
I see Heaven's glories shine
And Faith shines equal arming
me from Fear

Although the poems are short, and seemingly simple, they reveal a unique vision of the world. Their beauty and intensity catches the reader by surprise. Emily Brontë was able to generalize her personal vision so that all her readers could share in it.

In 1848 Branwell died. Charlotte, Emily, and Anne all took sick at his funeral. Emily quickly wasted away from consumption but she would not speak of her illness. The day before she died she dressed and fed her dogs as usual. An hour before her death, lying on the dining room sofa, she told Charlotte that she could now send for the doctor. But it was too late. Her dog Keeper followed the mourning family into the church where Emily was buried in the family tomb; Keeper continued to sleep on the floor outside of her bedroom every night. Emily's death was soon followed by that of her sister Anne. That left only Charlotte, who continued to write and live with her father. Charlotte enjoyed her growing literary fame and her contacts with members of the literary world, such as Elizabeth Gaskell, who wrote her biography after her death. Charlotte wed and died within a year. The father continued living for many years.

Emily's talents, her unique character, shine through in her beautiful drawings of nature (especially of her beloved dogs), in her poems, and her magnificent novel. *Wuthering Heights* has inspired subsequent generations of writers, musicians, actors, and screenwriters, who have used *Wuthering Heights* as the inspiration for their own works. Thus each generation has re-created *Wuthering Heights* for itself, finding new meaning in this fascinating novel.

WUTHERING HEIGHTS

The first item that may throw the reader of this book off balance is its title. No one outside of the local people of Yorkshire, England, uses the word, "wuthering." "Wuthering Heights," the narrator of the novel explains, "is the name of Mr. Heathcliff's dwelling. 'Wuthering' being a significant provincial adjective, descriptive of the atmospheric tumult to which its station is exposed in stormy weather." Thus little vegetation can grow in the windy area where Wuthering Heights is located. This isolated and bleak setting provides the perfect background for the characters of *Wuthering Heights*.

It is not stated where the action of *Wuthering Heights* occurs, but from much evidence (Yorkshire accents, physical descriptions), it would seem to be set near the town of Haworth where the Brontës lived. Many people believe that an old abandoned building near Haworth called Top Withens was the model for Wuthering Heights. This is an area that is not by the sea, but near a river, in rural, northeast England.

One of the interesting things about *Wuthering Heights* is how insular it feels. There are so few characters, and the names of the characters in the first generation are repeated among the characters in the second generation. Catherine Earnshaw Linton gives birth to a daughter named Catherine; even Heathcliff is named for a child who died. And almost all of the characters are related to each other. The town of Gimmerton seems far away. Although the doctor and the lawyer are called in and Heathcliff and Isabella both move away for a while, all of the action of *Wuthering Heights* takes place at the Heights, Thrushcross

Grange, or on the moors. This insularity can lead to some confusion (both for the reader and for strangers like Lockwood who happen into the story); for the sake of convenience we will refer to the mother as Cathy, and the daughter as Catherine.

CHARACTERS

Heathcliff. He has only one name which serves as both his first and last names, and he was named for a child of the Earnshaws that died in infancy. Heathcliff is the central character in *Wuthering Heights*. He is a boy when Mr. Earnshaw brings him home from Liverpool. He appears dark, different from the other children; he may be of Irish or of gypsy descent. And he is an intruder into the world of Wuthering Heights. Perhaps because Mr. Earnshaw favors him, the other children don't like him at first. He is demanding from the beginning, taking Hindley's horse when his own horse goes lame. Yet, when Mr. Earnshaw dies and Hindley begins to

vent his jealous dislike of him, Cathy begins to like him. Together, Heathcliff and Catherine conspire to fight against those who represent authority—Hindley and Joseph. Hindley not only denies Heathcliff an equal opportunity for education within the family, but eventually forces him to work as a stableboy (see previ-

ous page). In time, Cathy comes to see him as Hindley wants her to: as unrefined and socially inferior. The bond that was forged between them when they were children is loosened. It isn't gone, however: in the most famous scene in the novel Cathy claims that Heathcliff "...is more myself than I am. Whatever our souls

A Romantic Hero

Wuthering Heights owes much to the Romantic novels that Emily Brontë read as a child. Indeed, Heathcliff, like sister Charlotte's character Mr. Rochester from *Jane Eyre*, emerges from the tradition of Goethe's *Young Werther*, and from the brilliant and flamboyant model of the "byronic" hero, Lord Byron himself. Heathcliff *is* dark, handsome, mysterious; certainly that's how Isabella sees him. He is attuned to, and aligned with, the landscape and weather in the book: the dark settings, both in the old houses and on the moors, have a romantic and gothic feel to them which heightens the romantic appeal. Even the weather at times is in accord with the emotions of the characters: for example, when Heathcliff run away from Wuthering Heights, it rains wildly. These images

heighten Heathcliff's aura of romantic mystery. And in addition to literature, Emily had one other source of inspiration for Heathcliff: her brother Branwell, whose self-destructive, sometimes brutish behavior is mirrored in Heathcliff, in Rochester, and in Anne Brontë's Arthur Huntington from *The Tenant of Wildfell Hall*. Heathcliff, of the three, is the most striking and fantastic of these brooding heroes, and would in turn inspire dozens, if not hundreds, of similarly dark, troubled, heroes in twentieth century romantic fiction. But Emily Brontë only drew on the examples of literature and her brother's life to enrich her portrait. Heathcliff transcends, through his passion, his violence and his love, any source or inspiration to become a wholly original creation.

are made of, his and mine are the same, and Linton's is as different as a moonbeam from lightning, or frost from fire." When he overhears Cathy say that she could never marry him, Heathcliff disappears. When he returns a few years later he has somehow acquired both money and social polish. Then he begins his revenge, acquiring the legal rights to Wuthering Heights and the Grange, and destroying Hindley and Isabella in the process. He kidnaps young Catherine and forces her to marry his son. But his attempt to destroy Hindley's son, Hareton, is not so successful. Heathcliff realizes the intrinsic worth of this boy who he has attempted to degrade as he was degraded. It is possibly his respect for this boy, and not his passion for Cathy, that gives a positive note to Heathcliff's character. Heathcliff is a romantic character who retains some of our sympathy despite the baseness of his actions, and he spends the rest of the novel trying to be rejoined with Cathy, to enjoy once again the bond they had as children.

Catherine Earnshaw, called **Cathy**. She is a wild and passionate child who grows up spoiled and without supervision; she expects that she can have everything she wants. After Heathcliff and Cathy look through a window at Thrushcross Grange, Cathy wants the kind of life she sees there. From that moment she begins to favor Edgar Linton over Heathcliff. When Cathy tries to explain to Nelly her very different feelings for Heathcliff and Edgar, she cries to Nelly that "I *am* Heathcliff," yet she feels that she cannot marry Heathcliff. Although they have the same soul, in worldly terms he is beneath her: the bond between Cathy and Heathcliff is spiritual rather than earthly. Indeed, when she marries Edgar Linton, she is hoping that she can have the luxury of the Grange and keep her relationship with Heathcliff as well; in this, of course, she is wrong. Cathy rules over her husband, who tries not to upset her and bring out her passionate nature. When she finds she cannot keep both Heathcliff and Edgar she dies giving birth to her daughter, Catherine.

Hindley Earnshaw. Cathy's brother. As a young man Hindley is extremely jealous of Heathcliff, and seizes every opportunity to torment him; but Heathcliff keeps him in line by threatening to tell his father of his bad behavior. After his father's death, Hindley comes home from college with a wife, Frances, and banishes Heathcliff to a life as a servant. Hindley and Frances object to Cathy's closeness with someone who is outside of their social station. When his wife Frances dies in childbirth, Hindley turns to dissipation, and gives charge of his son Hareton over to Nelly (Hindley's attachment to, and grief for, his wife is almost the only good we see of him). When Heathcliff returns to Wuthering Heights after being away for years he begins his revenge on Hindley, taking advantage of Hindley's love of drink and gambling to win the deed to Wuthering Heights for himself, and to win charge of Hareton as well.

Ellen Dean, called **Nelly**. One of the book's narrators, Nelly is practi-

cally a member of the Earnshaw family. She was brought up with Hindley Earnshaw, and is an intimate in much of the action, and influences the action several times. For example, she does not tell Cathy that Heathcliff is listening when Cathy discusses Edgar Linton with her. Later, she allows Heathcliff to see Cathy while she is dying. She also nurses Hareton, Hindley's son, and has been in charge of Catherine for most of her life. She is held at Wuthering Heights by Heathcliff when he kidnaps Catherine.

Catherine Linton, called **Catherine**. She is the daughter of Cathy and Edgar Linton. A lovely, energetic, and pampered young lady, she is brought up by her father and Nelly in the luxury of Thrushcross Grange. She knows almost nothing about her family history, and does not leave the limits of Thrushcross Grange until she is thirteen years old. She has met her cousin Linton Heathcliff once, and later Heathcliff uses her curiosity about him to

kidnap her and force her to marry him. As Linton is on his deathbed when they wed, Catherine is more of a nurse than a wife. After his death she remains at the Heights. At the end of the novel, however, she has found happiness in teaching and being with her future husband, Hareton Earnshaw.

Edgar Linton.

Cathy first sees Edgar fighting with his sister over a puppy, and thinks him ridiculous. As they grow up Cathy comes to admire Edgar for his kindness, his intelligence, and his difference from herself. He, in turn, is entranced by Cathy's energy and beauty. In the wake of the intimacy created by his first fight with Cathy, they agree to marry. Edgar attempts to keep the peace in his family by giving in to his wife's whims, but Heathcliff is the bane of his life. He tries unsuccessfully to stop Cathy's relationship with Heathcliff after Heathcliff returns from his years away. When Cathy dies, Edgar is saddened, but takes delight in his daughter. While Edgar is dying, Heathcliff kidnaps his daughter so that he is unable to see her before he dies. Edgar does not have time before he dies to change his will in order to stop Heathcliff from exacting revenge on the second generation.

Isabella Linton.

Like her brother, Isabella grew up in the cultured atmosphere of Thrushcross Grange. She falls in love with Heathcliff because she believes him to be a romantic character, and she doesn't believe Cathy when Cathy tells her the truth about him. Her life after running away with Heathcliff is tragic. She has a child with him, but Heathcliff abuses her and makes her life a living hell (he even tries to hang her dog on the way out of the garden during their elopement). She explains in a letter to her brother that she has left Heathcliff, taking baby Linton with her. Heathcliff doesn't pursue her (he has his own agenda at Wuthering Heights) but when she dies he immediately claims his son, Linton Heathcliff

ISABELLA THEN CRIED OUT . . .

I LOVE HIM MORE THAN YOU EVER LOVED EDGAR! AND HE MIGHT LOVE ME IF YOU WOULD LET HIM!

I WOULDN'T BE YOU FOR A KINGDOM, THEN! YOU DON'T KNOW HEATHCLIFF LIKE I DO . . . HE IS A FIERCE, WOLFISH MAN! HE'D BE QUITE CAPABLE OF MARRYING YOU FOR YOUR FORTUNE AND EXPECTATIONS!

Linton Heathcliff.

Linton Heathcliff is the sickly son of Isabella and Heathcliff. Heathcliff cannot understand how he, a man of passion and vitality, could have fathered such a son! He takes the view that since Linton is going to die anyway, he might as well take advantage of the boy's selfish and complaining nature to use him to his own advantage. Thus Heathcliff forces his son's marriage to Catherine in order to secure his own right to the property of Thrushcross Grange.

Furniture

There's a good deal of hiding and lurking about in Wuthering Heights, and in keeping with the old cliche, the people who eavesdrop do not always hear things that make them happy. One pivotal hiding place in the book is lost on modern readers, because we're not acquainted with the piece of furniture Brontë mentions. Cathy is in the kitchen telling Nelly that to marry Heathcliff would degrade her.

Heathcliff is not precisely hidden, but resting on a bench behind a settle, a high-backed wooden bench with high arms meant to block out drafts. Settles were generally placed before the fire, where they screened the fire from drafts and kept the settle's occupant nicely warm. But that same shielding action prevents Cathy from seeing Heathcliff—or the effect his declaration has on her.

Hareton Earnshaw. When we first meet Hareton he is a rude, dirty lad. Although he is the son of Hindley Earnshaw, and is raised during his early years by Nelly, on his father's death he is left to be raised by Heathcliff. Once, in a drunken stupor, Hareton's father drops Hareton from a balcony and he is caught by Heathcliff; this act symbolizes the boy's fate, dumped by his father into Heathcliff's fold.

Heathcliff's original idea is to make the boy as bad as he is by raising him in the same way, so Heathcliff keeps Hareton unlearned and unwashed. Yet some greater mettle shows in Hareton, a finer nature that leads him to learn to read on his own,

YOU'RE WORSE THAN A HEATHEN!

and eventually to respond to Catherine's gestures of friendship with his own, until he is able to love and woo her. Hareton has the ability to make the people around him better than they are: he brings out the best in Joseph, Heathcliff, and Catherine.

Joseph. Joseph acts as something like a tragic Greek chorus in *Wuthering Heights*. He speaks in Yorkshire dialect, sometimes difficult for us as readers to understand. Quoting the Bible, he predicts hellfire and damnation for everyone around him. Joseph is called a "Methodist," although he may not be a member of that church, for his dour and unforgiving manner. Like Heathcliff, however, Joseph thinks well of Hareton Earnshaw.

Nelly calls him "the wearisomest, self-righteous pharisee that ever ransacked a Bible to rake the promises to himself, and fling the curses on his neighbours." Joseph may show something of the low esteem in which Emily Brontë held organized religion.

Lockwood. The tenant Heathcliff finds for Thrushcross Grange. In chronological terms Lockwood comes onto the scene late in *Wuthering Heights*. He has rented the Grange from Heathcliff and visits the area at the beginning of the novel and at the end. Lockwood tries to be urbane, he believes he is misanthropic, yet he is frequently looking for company. Lockwood cannot show his feelings: we learn that he was once attracted to a woman, but the minute she started to like him, he ran away. At first he fancies that Catherine may be interested in him, but after hearing her story he fears she will be too much like her mother, and he shies away. Lockwood is, as Heathcliff points out to him, unhappy in many of his conjectures, and yet he stands for the reader, asking questions the reader might want to ask, and sorting through the complex tangle of family and relationships at Wuthering Heights.

NARRATION

The story of *Wuthering Heights* is started by Lockwood, continued by Cathy's journals, related by Nelly Dean to Lockwood, and filled out by letters and the reports of minor characters. Many readers construct charts to help them understand the twists

and turns of the events, years, characters, as the story is not chronologically. It's importan remember that none of the peo who tell, or comment on, the st Heathcliff, the Earnshaws, and t Lintons, is without opinions and udices in the matter. The reader i sort out the story for him or, herse

PLOT

The plot of *Wuthering Heights* can be divided in halves between the action at Wuthering Heights and the action at the Grange. It is also chronologically divided in the middle by the death of Cathy, the birth of her daughter, Catherine, and the emergence of the second generation in the second half of the book. One way to look at the action is to see it as the process of Catherine Earnshaw (Cathy) becoming Catherine Heathcliff (spiritually) and Catherine Linton (by marriage); and, in the second half of the story, Catherine Linton (daughter of Cathy Linton) becoming Catherine Heathcliff (by marriage) and ultimately Catherine Earnshaw (when she marries Hareton Earnshaw on New Year's day, after the novel's end).

Wuthering Heights begins with the date "1801" and moves from the present to the past and back again. At the beginning the narrator, Lockwood, has rented Thrushcross Grange from Heathcliff and goes to visit his landlord at Wuthering Heights, where he meets the characters living there— Heathcliff, Catherine, Hareton

Inspiration

How did a clergyman's daughter living an isolated existence come up with this novel? Emily Brontë was, after all, a reserved woman who made few friends and communicated rarely outside of her own home. The idea for her novel came from her own imagination. She had practiced creating imaginary places and melodramatic characters in her writings about Gondal. She had expressed deep emotions in her poetry. Although she had witnessed the emotional excesses of her brother Branwell, with his unfortunate love affair, his drinking and opium-taking, she had never been close to a person as far outside of the normal range as Heathcliff. While the novels and poetry she read might have enriched her imaginings, they were not the "source" of Heathcliff or any other of the characters she created.

Brontë's imagination in turn has inspired many others, writers, musicians, and movie makers. The classic 1939 movie takes great liberties with the plot as written by Emily Brontë, but it has done much to popularize the story. Those who have seen this version of *Wuthering Heights* can never forget Laurence Olivier in the role of Heathcliff, yet his portrayal of Heathcliff is very different from the character created by Emily Brontë. Several more recent movies have been made from this novel as well, each with its own interpretation of Heathcliff.

Earnshaw, and Joseph—and tries to make sense of this dysfunctional household. On his second visit to Wuthering Heights, Lockwood is snowed in, becoming almost a captive, and forced to spend the night. While in bed he reads the names scratched on the window; Catherine Earnshaw, Catherine Heathcliff, Catherine Linton. Then he reads the diaries of this young woman, Cathy Earnshaw, detailing her childhood friendship with Heathcliff. Heathcliff has been cast out of the family at the death of Mr. Earnshaw, and works as a stable boy for Hindley, who has long hated Heathcliff for usurping the affection that should have been his. Cathy and Heathcliff enjoy the moors together, rebelling against the adults in the house. Lockwood falls asleep and wakes to hear a noise at the window and a voice calling to him to let her in. "It's twenty years, I've been a waif for twenty years." The ghost identifies herself as Catherine Linton (Cathy's name when she died) and holds his arm with a deadly grasp. In his terror, Lockwood rubs the wrist of this ghost against the broken window glass until its blood soaks the sheets. His frightened screams bring Heathcliff to the scene. Heathcliff opens the window and calls for this ghost to enter. Rather than being frightened, Heathcliff eagerly seeks contact with this spirit. Lockwood returns with relief to the Grange, where he asks Nelly Dean about the people he has met and their histories.

Nelly tells Lockwood of the youth of the Earnshaw children: how Heathcliff was brought into the house, and how, after the death of Mr. Earnshaw, Heathcliff and Cathy formed such a strong bond with each other. When Heathcliff comes home without Cathy from a romp on the moors, he tells Nelly that they were looking through the window of Thrushcross Grange and a dog attacked Cathy, and that she was brought inside by the Lintons. The Lintons nurse Cathy back to health. When she returns from Thrushcross Grange Cathy has changed: she sees Heathcliff as dirty and unrefined, and she yearns to

enjoy a more elegant way of life. But her temper has not become more ladylike—in a passion when circumstances make her choose between Heathcliff and Edgar Linton, Cathy slaps Nelly, shakes the baby Hareton, and strikes Edgar, all in the course of a short afternoon. Eventually she decides to marry Edgar, but tells Nelly "I've no more business to marry Edgar Linton than I have to be in heaven." Yet Cathy feels it would degrade her to marry Heathcliff. Heathcliff overhears part of this conversation, is bitterly hurt, and rushes out. Although Cathy tries to find Heathcliff, he has disappeared. She goes forward with her marriage, and Heathcliff remains absent for three years.

When Heathcliff returns he is wealthy and superficially cultured. He establishes himself at Wuthering Heights, aiding Hindley's disintegration by encouraging his drinking and gambling. This is all part of

Heathcliff's revenge: he has determined to be the owner of Wuthering Heights, and gives Hindley a mortgage on the property which will allow it to fall into his hands should Hindley die. After establishing himself at the Heights, he turns his sights on Thrushcross Grange. Heathcliff now appears to be such a gentleman that Nelly does not recognize him when he arrives there. He visits Cathy at Thrushcross Grange and begins to court Isabella, but Edgar takes a firm stand and throws Heathcliff out of his house. The conflict between Edgar and Heathcliff will lead to Cathy's illness and eventual death. In this event we see that Nelly tells the story but is also an actor in it: Nelly does not believe that Cathy is really ill, and consequently she does not inform Edgar of her condition.

Heathcliff and Isabella run off together. Isabella tells the story in a letter that she writes to Nelly: Heathcliff tried to kill Isabella's dog as they eloped,

ONE DAY, ELLEN, LOOKING OUT TO THE COURT FROM THE KITCHEN WINDOW, SAW

PLEASE, HEATHCLIFF, NOT OUT HERE IN THE COURT! MY BROTHER WILL BE FURIOUS!

HOWEVER, CONTRARY TO ELLEN'S BELIEF, CATHY WAS DESPERATELY ILL. SHE WAS IN GRAVE DANGER OF LOSING HER MIND. THE COUNTY DOCTOR WAS CALLED AND KEPT WATCH OVER HER ALL THAT NIGHT . . .

and now he abuses and mistreats his wife. Returned to live at Wuthering Heights, Heathcliff leaves Isabella at home and goes to the Grange to see Cathy. He finds her on her deathbed and they kiss passionately for the first—and only—time. Catherine is born that night and her mother, Cathy, dies. Heathcliff hopes Cathy will not go to heaven when she dies but will haunt him instead: "Be with me always—take any form— drive me mad! only *do* not leave me in this abyss, where I cannot find you!" He spends his years after Cathy's death seeking Cathy.

After Cathy's death, Isabella takes her son, Linton, and escapes from Heathcliff; she has no contact with her brother for twelve years or so. Edgar Linton and his daughter, Catherine, lead a quiet life until Isabella asks him to take her son, Linton, as she is dying. He does, but as soon as Heathcliff hears of Isabella's death, he comes for Linton. By now, Heathcliff plans to extend his revenge by becoming the owner of

AT THAT, HE CRIED OUT IN ANGUISH . . .

CATHERINE EARNSHAW, MAY YOU NOT REST AS LONG AS I AM LIVING! BE WITH ME ALWAYS . . . TAKE MY FORM . . . DRIVE ME MAD! DON'T LEAVE ME IN THE ABYSS WHERE I CANNOT FIND YOU! I CANNOT LIVE WITHOUT MY LIFE! I CANNOT LIVE WITHOUT MY SOUL!

Thrushcross Grange as well as Wuthering Heights. Catherine is a sheltered thirteen-year-old who has never been outside the area surrounding Thrushcross Grange. By exciting her curiosity about the Heights and her cousin, Heathcliff is able to entice Catherine to visit Linton at Wuthering Heights. Once he has her inside the house, Heathcliff kidnaps Catherine. He entraps Catherine into marrying Linton, and Linton dies soon after. While Catherine is at Wuthering Heights, her father, Edgar, dies at Thrushcross Grange.

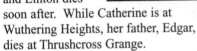

We have come full circle, around to the beginning scenes of *Wuthering Heights*. This is the point at which Lockwood first visits Wuthering Heights. Nelly then tells him the rest of the story. Trapped at Wuthering Heights, Catherine rebels for a while, and slowly forms an alliance with Hareton. We learn that they are soon to marry and live at Thrushcross Grange. At the end of *Wuthering Heights* Heathcliff dies, hoping to be united for eternity with Cathy. Although she was buried next to Edgar in the cemetery, Heathcliff has the side of her coffin removed, and will have the side of his own removed as well, so that their remains can mingle after death. Catherine and Hareton will be married on the first day of the new year, and we hope it will usher in a new era for the inhabitants of Wuthering Heights and Thrushcross Grange.

THEMES AND ISSUES

Why doesn't Cathy marry Heathcliff?

Setting aside issues of class, money, and snobbery, this question has plagued readers for more than a hundred years. This is not a novel about a great, missed opportunity. Everything would *not* have been all right had Cathy and Heathcliff married—it would just be a completely different story. In truth, a marriage of Cathy and Heathcliff would border on incest; although they are not physically related, they have been raised as siblings. They are close spiritually, like different parts of the same person, sharing the same soul. Cathy hopes that by marrying Edgar Linton she will be able to raise Heathcliff to her own level, and that she will be able to enjoy both men in different ways. However, neither Heathcliff nor Edgar can abide this plan.

Spiritual love vs. physical love.

For all the romance of *Wuthering Heights*, there is little sex. Cathy and Isabella do end up with babies, but there's no sense of process: the statement that a baby was born is almost the only thing we hear of the subject—readers may be pardoned if they're suprised to find that Cathy's terminal illness was complicated by pregnancy! The whole effect is rather magical, as if one could get a baby by waving a wand. But by the end of the novel Catherine and Hareton are touching and kissing, in the first instance of physical love that is not laced with sadism.

Some people have argued whether Heathcliff and Cathy were more than good friends. Indeed, some ask, is it not possible that Heathcliff is the father of Catherine? (And if so, what would that say about Catherine's marriage to Heathcliff's son Linton?) But, their relationship prior to Heathcliff's departure doesn't *look* like a sexual one. Heathcliff and Cathy *are* intimately connected, but the bond is of a spiritual nature. Cathy has her baby six months after Heathcliff returns, and we are told it is a seven-months baby, so he could not be the father. But in many ways this spiritual bond between Cathy and Heathcliff is stronger than the physical, sexual relationship between Cathy and her husband, Edgar Linton. It is in the afterlife, when they are dead, that Heathcliff plans to be close to Cathy; thus he calls to her spirit to enter Wuthering Heights and removes the sides of their coffins so that their dust can mingle. A shepherd boy at the very end tells Lockwood that there is a report of a

ghostly couple roaming the moors together. Lockwood can't believe it, as the graveyard seems so still to him: but he has been wrong in his assumptions before.

Heathcliff's Revenge.

Heathcliff seeks revenge against Hindley for treating him badly during his boyhood at Wuthering Heights. He accomplishes his purpose by taking advantage of Hindley's penchant for gambling and drinking, eventually usurping Hindley's place as the head of the family at Wuthering Heights. Heathcliff probably acts within the law, although some readers have speculated that he may have hastened Hindley's end by smothering him with a pillow. Heathcliff also seeks revenge on Edgar Linton because Edgar has married Cathy. He takes this revenge by marrying Edgar's sister Isabella and making her miserable, and at the same time, wounds Cathy by marrying another woman. Heathcliff and Cathy's relationship is composed of the extremes of emotion: it encompasses both love and hate, and neither Cathy nor Heathcliff can rest easily until both are dead. In this revenge, he goes beyond the grave; in his revenge against Hindley and Edgar he goes beyond the law. He kidnaps Catherine and forces her to marry his son, Linton. By contriving this marriage,

The Brontë Society

What do Elvis, Mickey Mouse, the Brontë Sisters and Nine Inch Nails have in common? They all have fan clubs!

Perhaps The Brontë Society would feel that the term "fan club" lacks dignity or falls short of stating their mission. But the Society, founded in 1893, basically works to collect and spread information about the Brontë Sisters and their works, and to encourage discussion of the Brontës and their work by teachers, students, and, yes, *fans*. The Society owns the Parsonage at Haworth, in Yorkshire, which it runs as a museum, with rooms furnished as they might have been during their lifetimes, displays of the sisters' personal belongings, sketches and writings, and a variety of educational programs. The Society runs writing and art workshops at various times of the year, as well as workshops for teachers. The Society also has a junior auxiliary: The Angrians, for Brontë enthusiasts under 14!

If you can't make it to England, you can find the Brontë Society on the World Wide Web, at: **virtual pc.com/bpmweb/bpeduc.htm**. Aside from membership applications and schedules of events at the Brontë Parsonage Museum, there are photos of the Parsonage itself, and reproductions of some of the sisters' sketches. And don't feel you have to stop at the Parsonage. As of the time of publication, a search of the internet yielded more than 600 sites that mention Emily Brontë (though not all of them are in English, and not all of them discuss Brontë or her work in depth). Many of the sites are maintained by people who simply love Emily's writing—particularly *Wuthering Heights*—and want to share that love with readers—maybe you!

Heathcliff is assured that he will own Thrushcross Grange: the property will be transferred to Catherine when her father dies, then to her husband (as a married woman's property became her husband's). When the ailing Linton dies, as Heathcliff knows he soon will, the property will go, not to his wife, but to his father. At that point Heathcliff owns both Wuthering Heights and Thrushcross Grange. It is only at the very end of the novel that Heathcliff loses his taste for revenge and does not fight the burgeoning love between Catherine and Hareton.

Heathcliff's Evil

Many times during this novel, Heathcliff is compared to Satan. But is he really evil? It is impossible to know. What *is* interesting is that almost everyone is attracted to him.

Mr. Earnshaw brings him home, Cathy forms a bond with him, Nelly comes to like him, Isabella finds herself attracted to him, Lockwood thinks himself similar to Heathcliff. Heathcliff never waivers in his love for Cathy, which is an attractive trait. Yet he does some horrible things along the way, and he destroys Isabella and his son Linton. However, he is not successful in destroying Hareton, and he does not have the power to combat the growing relationship between Hareton and Catherine. Heathcliff's clear-sighted respect for Hareton may be his most redeeming characteristic.

STUDY QUESTIONS

•Where are the ghosts? In the novel we find the ghost of Cathy visiting Lockwood while he sleeps at Wuthering Heights, and Heathcliff desperately seeking to reunite with this vision. At the end of the novel, after the death of Heathcliff, local people report sightings of a ghostly couple, but Lockwood wonders "how any one could ever imagine unquiet slumbers for the sleepers in that quiet earth." Now that they are joined in death, should Heathcliff and Cathy at last lie quiet, or are these restless spirits doomed to wander the moors forever?

•Which character do you like the best? Which least? Whom would you like to give advice to? What would that advice be?

•Are the Yorkshire moors a "character" in Wuthering Heights? Weather often echoes the emotional impact of a given scene, but does the landscape itself comment on or heighten the impact of a given scene? Can you link characters to different landscapes? For example, Linton tells Catherine "the pleasantest manner of spending a hot July day was lying from morning till evening on a bank of heath in the middle of the moors, with the bees humming dreamingly about among the bloom." Contrast this with Heathcliff's or Cathy's feelings for the moors.

•Is the ending satisfying? Some critics are unhappy that Heathcliff loses resolve at the end and gives up on his revenge when he sees Catherine and Hareton together. Some feel a reasserting of the old, traditional order. Some dislike the fact that the spiritual gives way to the more earthly. Do *you* find the ending to the novel satisfying? Why?

About the Essayist:

Abigail Burnham Bloom holds a Ph.D. in English Literature from NYU. Dr. Bloom has taught at Rutgers University, NYU, and the New School for Social Research. She held a Post-Doctoral Fellowship in Victorian Literature at New York University, and is the Managing Editor of *Victorian Literature and culture.*